100 WAYS TO LOVE YOUR Daughter

Other Books by Matt and Lisa Jacobson

100 WAYS TO LOVE YOUR Daughter

THE SIMPLE, POWERFUL PATH TO A CLOSE AND LASTING RELATIONSHIP

MATT AND LISA JACOBSON

Revell

a division of Baker Publishing Group
Grand Rapids, Michigan

Published by Revell
a division of Baker Publishing Group
PO Box 6287, Grand Rapids, MI 49516-6287
www.revellbooks.com

Printed in the United States of America

Library of Congress Cataloging-in-Publication Data
Names: Jacobson, Matt, author. | Jacobson, Lisa, author.
Title: 100 ways to love your daughter : the simple, powerful path to a
    close and lasting relationship / Matt L. Jacobson and Lisa Jacobson.
Other titles: One hundred ways to love your daughter
Description: Grand Rapids, Michigan : Revell, a division of Baker
    Publishing Group, 2020.
Identifiers: LCCN 2019039125 | ISBN 9780800736668 (paperback)
Subjects: LCSH: Parent and child—Religious aspects—Christianity.
    | Daughters. | Child rearing—Religious aspects—Christianity. |
    Parenting—Religious aspects—Christianity.
Classification: LCC BV4529 .J33 2020 | DDC 248.8/45—dc23
LC record available at https://lccn.loc.gov/2019039125

20   21   22   23   24   25   26   7   6   5   4   3   2   1

In keeping with biblical principles of creation stewardship, Baker Publishing Group advocates the responsible use of our natural resources. As a member of the Green Press Initiative, our company uses recycled paper when possible. The text paper of this book is composed in part of post-consumer waste.

INTRODUCTION

How can you cultivate and keep a close, loving relationship with your daughter? Whatever her age, how can you reach and hold on to her heart through the years? Perhaps she's young and you already have her heart, but how will you keep it as she grows older? You desire the best for her, but how do you translate that love into a relationship that will endure?

This book is a resource for what to do, what to say, and how to treat daughters of all ages. For you to maintain a continuous, growing relationship with her, she needs to know and experience your love—and that is the reason for this book. Just read one entry per day, consider it, and then apply it to your relationship with her.

Sometimes we need to change what we think. Sometimes we need to change what we say (and how we say it!). And sometimes we need to change what we do. For some parents, it's a minor adjustment. For others, it will be a dramatic reform. But for all parents, it's the journey of loving your daughter better each day as you are learning to love her well—the foundation of a meaningful, trusting relationship that will stand the test of time as she becomes a woman.

We are the parents of eight awesome children, including four girls ages nineteen to twenty-four. We've walked this journey and are still making it with you. We haven't always done it right and hope you find us to be transparent about our mistakes, but we are grateful to enjoy close, loving relationships with our girls. Wherever you are on this journey, learning to love your daughter well is the path to all that's best in your relationship with her today and in the future.

Matt & Lisa Jacobson

Ask her
REAL QUESTIONS.

Close. That's how our friend describes our relationship with our daughters. And it's true, we are close. We laugh and hug and talk about most everything. So how did we get there? How did we grow so close?

This kind of closeness comes from seeking—from seeking their hearts and pursuing a relationship. It comes from being interested in their thoughts, fears, hopes, and dreams.

And it comes from asking questions.

We ask our daughters questions most every day. We wonder how they're doing, what they're thinking about, and how they're feeling.

Our girls need us to ask them about these things. They won't necessarily volunteer what's on their hearts and minds. They need us to ask, and they need us to care about their answers.

Your daughter needs you to ask her too.

Get up early
AND WATCH THE SUNRISE
together.

Another week begins. It's time to get to work, the gym, that event. The demands won't lighten up and neither will the speed of your daughter's growth and maturity. Time will race by, and she'll be out the door and off to the next phase of her life with lightning speed. There will never be a convenient time to slow down and just "be" with your daughter. There's just too much to do.

And yet, somehow, busy, wise parents find the time.

How? If we're honest, every one of us has time for those things that are truly important to us. In fact, that's what we've already done, whether we're the parent who pauses to enjoy God's handiwork with our daughter or the parent who never takes the time. Both types of parents have prioritized what is important. Which one are you?

Love your daughter by elevating her over the demands of your schedule—by anticipating the natural beauty of a sunrise or sunset or some other scene that says, "Let's take a few minutes to share God's creation together."

A close relationship with your daughter is built by finding and sharing those moments together.

Give her
A WARM HUG.

She walked into the room, and since I'm her mom, I could tell she was worked up before she even reached me. It probably had nothing to do with me, but I sensed that I would suffer the brunt of it all the same. Before she really got going, however, I had the sudden inspiration to reach out and give her a hug—not a quick obligatory hug either, but a slow, deliberate, no-agenda embrace.

I think we were both somewhat surprised at that moment. But the impact on her spirit—and on our relationship—was undeniable. Whatever it was that had been eating at her seemed to slip away.

Sometimes your girl doesn't need words or instruction or correction as much as she simply needs your caring hug. So reach out and hug her tight today.

Write her
A LETTER.

When was the last time you received a handwritten letter, or even a typed one? How did it make you feel? Letters are increasingly uncommon, and chances are it's been a long time (never?) since you've written one. In this case, that's good news. When you write a letter, it will stand out and have a powerful impact. It will be something your daughter can cherish for life.

Writing can be intimidating, but your letter doesn't have to earn international literary acclaim. Honest thoughts are all that are necessary for a meaningful letter from your heart to hers.

Here are a few ideas to get you started:

- Tell her how proud of her you are.
- Tell her what you love about her personality.
- Tell her of your lifelong commitment to her.
- Tell her of your confidence in her and in her future.

Maybe purchase some special paper and an envelope, which will add to this heartfelt gift.

And another tip—write your rough draft on basic lined paper or type it out first. You might have a few changes to make before your final version is ready. Then write the final draft on your intended stationery.

If you have to send your letter, do so. If your daughter still lives at home, leave your letter someplace she will be sure to find it.

Be ready
TO HAPPILY serve HER.

You might consider our daughters spoiled once we share this.

Every morning since they were old enough to drink coffee (which in our house is embarrassingly young), their dad would make a pot of French-press coffee and serve them a cup the way each one liked it. A little splash of cream, the right amount of sugar, and in their own special cup. He never missed this daily ritual as long as he was home.

It might seem like he was spoiling them, but he always took such pleasure in serving them their coffee this way each morning. Handing them a sweet cup of coffee to start out their day was his way of saying, "I love you" without saying a single word.

Maybe your daughter doesn't drink coffee, but you have many other creative options and opportunities to serve her with a smile. Pick one of those ways and start serving her today.

6

Arrange FOR A *father-daughter* DATE.

Many dads are head over heels about their daughters. Ask them. They'll tell you.

"My little Karen is an amazing . . ."

"You should see Chloe when she . . ."

"Audrey is the most awesome . . ."

We may love our daughters, but sometimes the connection between how we feel and what we've communicated to them needs more focus. She is left to wonder what she really means to you. There's nothing like a daddy-daughter date to speak the answer to her question loud and clear: "Yes, you are a special, wonderful person—especially to me."

For our daughters to feel a sense of their own value, they need to know *we want to*, *we desire to*, and *we like to* spend time with them.

I have enjoyed some father-daughter dates with my girls over the years, and by God's grace, I have wonderful relationships with them. But, I can tell you, I wish I would have dated them far more than I did.

We dads need to push back on the pressures of life to make room for the relationships that really matter.

Give her OPPORTUNITIES TO *serve others.*

The call for help came in the middle of the day. This young mom was clearly in a tough circumstance and needed some advice. I recognized the desperate tone in her voice and told her I'd be over as soon as I could.

But what about her four young ones, plus a little baby? Who could stay with them on such short notice while she and I went out to talk it through? I approached one of my daughters and briefly explained the situation. She caught on right away and began filling her backpack with fun toys, a princess crown, and party whistles. In a few short minutes, she was packed and ready to go.

The children shyly stood back when we first arrived, but soon my friend and I were able to slip out to spend a tearful, healing conversation over a cup of tea. We returned to find my daughter playing a board game with my friend's children while the baby slept sweetly in her arms.

Surprising, yet not surprising. Wasn't it just yesterday that this little lady before me was sleeping sweetly in my own arms?

What a gift to show your girl how she can be a blessing to others by serving them well.

Prove to her
THAT YOU'RE HER
biggest fan.

Your influence over your daughter's sense of accomplishment and personal potential cannot be overstated. She will get the highest sense of confidence and motivation from your responses to her efforts, regardless of how young she is. Whether she's struggling to take her first steps, learning her letters, trying to finger paint, attempting to bake a cake for the first time, playing on a team, or learning to drive a car, your daughter's sense of courage to try new things grows from Dad and Mom cheering her on.

Every day contains opportunities to support her. You can believe in her before she even knows to believe in herself.

Life will provide endless voices that will seek to diminish your dear girl. So never miss an opportunity to cheer for her. And always remember, every young child who believes in herself had a parent who believed in her first.

TAKE A WALK
together.

Taking a walk together is such a simple thing. Yet there's something about the fresh air and side-by-side striding that can start some of the most amazing conversations.

If she's little, grab her hand and slowly—this can't be rushed—walk out the door together. Let her explore and take the time to look at all the interesting things along the way. Talk about God's creation and delight in observing it together.

If your girl is older, invite her to come along with you. And if this is a new activity for the two of you, begin with no agenda other than spending time outside together. Maybe you'll want to start out silently and let the conversation unfold naturally. You might find your daughter opens up more when she's not looking directly at you—and she'll be reassured to know you're right by her side.

Let her know that, just like this walk, you're on a journey together and there's nowhere else you'd rather be.

MAKE YOURSELF
available
TO HER.

Our friend was a fantastic provider. We had never seen a man work so hard with such powers of concentration. He was a machine—in the middle of the family room with everyone buzzing about, on vacation, at the office at night, up early in the morning—and his bank account echoed that fact.

Yeah, he was there, but he was never available. Although that was a few years ago.

This guy was on his way to being a millionaire then, and he's got a lot more money now. But if you were to go to his daughter's Facebook page, you wouldn't see a single picture of him—he's an irrelevancy, a ghost, a nonentity.

As parents, we never want this to be our story. And neither do our daughters. So make sure you're around and approachable when she's young and needs you.

And, when she's a little older, don't rush her off the end of your bed (as your eyes require toothpicks to keep them open) and out of your bedroom. Sometimes being available means not worrying about the time and listening patiently as she rambles on, "pouring it all out" until the wee hours.

Can you attend her recital, her game, her event? Your daughter spells differently than you do. She spells the word *love* this way: t-i-m-e. And remember, until your children are young adults, there's no such thing as quality time without quantity time. Quality time is a by-product of quantity time. Love your daughter by being available for her.

BE READY TO SAY
I'm sorry.

I've never been very good at apologizing. Maybe it was the way I was raised or perhaps it's my personality, but for some reason it's not easy for me to say. It doesn't mean I'm *not* sorry, only that I have a hard time finding the words.

But becoming a mom has given me plenty of opportunity to apologize, such as when I've lost my temper, said or done something hurtful, or simply let our children down. I've also had to realize that it's not enough to *be sorry* and move on—even if I do things differently going forward.

If I want to have an open relationship with my daughter, I have to humbly and clearly say I'm sorry when I've done her wrong. And then I must ask her to forgive me—without excuse or justification.

So go ahead and be ready to say you're sorry. She needs to hear those soft words from you.

Be patient
WITH THE
maturing process.

My twelve-year-old daughter stood in the Amsterdam airport. This was her first overseas experience, so I thought it would be a good teaching moment. "Okay, Sweetie, where is our gate?" She stood there, not moving or saying anything. I became frustrated, thinking she was being uncooperative (brilliant dad!). Then she looked at me with tears in her eyes and said, "Dad, I'm only twelve."

It was my turn for tears. I hugged her and asked her to forgive me.

Have you ever been impatient with the process?

We want our daughters to grow, to be strong, and to make their way in the world. We want the best for them, but sometimes what we desire turns too intense in a moment that needs gentleness and understanding. Like a beautiful apple blossom in early spring, your daughter stands before you with much potential, but maturity is a long way off. And just like that apple blossom, it takes time for fruit to grow, understanding to take hold, knowledge to increase, and wisdom to come into full measure.

There's no point in being impatient with apple blossoms, is there? They will mature as they need to. Your daughter is no different. Love her by being patient and gentle with her slow, steady progress to maturity.

Take the time
TO FULLY LISTEN TO
her heart.

As her mother, I probably should have guessed something was weighing on her heart, but in all honesty I didn't think this would be more than a casual conversation about the small details of her day. So I listened, nodded understandingly when appropriate, and then assumed we were about to wrap things up.

I tried not to appear impatient, as this entire process was taking some time, but I started feeling antsy to get on with my own day. And it was at that moment when she switched topics and suddenly dove down deep. I hadn't seen it coming, but, oh, am I so glad we went there. I'd had no idea she was struggling with such things, and I never would have known if I'd cut off the conversation too early.

A girl's heart cannot be rushed or squeezed in between a zillion other priorities. She needs her parent to be available to listen to her thoughts and concerns, her fears and insecurities, her hopes and dreams.

Communicate to your daughter that you're more than willing to sit and listen to whatever she wants to share with you. Give her your undivided attention and patiently listen to whatever she has to say—for however long it takes for her to say it.

Introduce her
TO A NEW SKILL.

Growing up in the interior of British Columbia, Canada, shooting guns was just a part of my, Matt's, life. We hunted moose every year ("BC Beef," everyone called it). Where we live now, owning and carrying firearms is also a part of life. I want my daughters to know how to shoot a gun responsibly and safely, and I've enjoyed the times we've shot clay pigeons with the 12-gauge or target practice with the .22s.

You may not come from a background that involves guns, but there are many other skills to teach your daughter. It could be anything. Teach her to throw a ball, read a map, navigate the airport (remember Amsterdam?). Teach her to use a computer, swim, paddle a canoe, kick a soccer ball, bait a hook and catch a fish. The options are endless.

You're not just giving her a new skill, you're giving her a piece of you—a piece of your heart. Relationships are built with hearts. Just remember not to be critical, demanding, or impatient, or she'll close her heart and not want to learn from you. But you already knew that, right?!

15

Encourage YOUR DAUGHTER IN HER INDIVIDUAL *fashion choices.*

We were all getting ready for our sons' karate tournament when our daughter walked into the room. She was wearing an elegant black dress, like something you'd wear to an evening gala . . . in, say, New York. Except we live in the famously casual Pacific Northwest.

A couple of her siblings came over to me and whispered, "Why is she wearing that, Mom? You have to make her change."

So I gently suggested that she might want to reconsider her wardrobe choice. But our elegant daughter insisted she wanted to wear the black dress. She didn't care if it was "unexpected" attire for an afternoon karate tournament; she liked this dress.

Later, this same daughter dyed her hair purple. Then red, then blonde, and currently "ice." You get the idea.

Perhaps you have a creative daughter as well. She doesn't share your same taste in fashion and has her own ideas instead. That's okay. Let her be "her" and give her permission to figure out her own style.

Remember, her heart is far more important than her outward appearance or unique fashion choices.

Celebrate
HER VICTORIES.

Did your daughter get an A on an assignment? Did she complete a difficult task? Did she hit a home run? Did she win some contest? Did she come in first at an event? Your daughter's life is going to be filled with "victory moments."

The world will never slow down, so you've got to decide early to celebrate those victories with her, whether big or small. Make the endless demands of life fit with your real priorities.

She accomplished something. Take a moment and find a meaningful way to acknowledge the milestone. Look ahead to the coming weeks and months. Is there something on the horizon you need to anticipate and be ready for? Celebrate your daughter's victories and let her know you are proud of the hard work she is doing.

SPEND TIME ON
your knees FOR HER.

Before becoming a mom, I never would have guessed what parenting would do for my prayer life.

My preconceived notion was that parenting was about making peanut butter sandwiches and tucking kids into bed at night. About kissing boo-boos and reminding the children to close the front door. About loving, correcting, supporting, cheering, and then loving them some more.

But I can see now that parenting is also a whole lot about prayer.

And for a while I thought it was just *me*. You know, like I wasn't doing this mothering business right or I wasn't quite enough or . . . *something*. I often threw myself down on my knees, calling out to God with a heart cry to keep her safe—and hopefully thriving—in this sometimes dark and dangerous world.

So, whether you're a seasoned parent or a brand-new one, let me encourage you that your prayers will have a powerful impact on your daughter—both now and for the rest of her life.

You'll find that some of your best parenting happens when you're humbly down on your knees.

Demonstrate
YOUR LOYALTY
to her.

As a father, I feel I should admit something that makes my heart hurt. When I look back on several situations with my daughters, I realize I was too evenhanded when it came to conflict with others. Because I didn't want to be seen as favoring my daughters unduly (like absolutely every other parent I've ever encountered—no exaggeration), I overcompensated.

The Bible tells us we aren't supposed to show favoritism (James 2:1). And I certainly didn't—to a fault. I misapplied this teaching, and looking back, the fact is that many times I was an adjudicator when I should have been a partisan.

Trust me, your daughter needs a partisan.

Don't make the mistake I did and treat every altercation with moral equivalency. Take your daughter's side and sort out the details later. If you don't, she won't feel protected. I've cried over this error. It makes me sick to remember, but I must own my mistakes.

I've asked my daughters for forgiveness. Learn from me so you won't have to walk the same path. Demonstrate to your daughter your clear loyalty.

Infuse hope
INTO YOUR
daughter's life.

Our youngest daughter suffered a massive stroke before she was even born and has faced more than her share of challenges. The brain damage was so severe, we had to tube-feed her for the first three years of her life since she couldn't swallow.

The medical staff told us that if she didn't learn to swallow as a baby, she'd never be able to. I didn't want to believe it, but those voices were strong. Her dad, on the other hand, refused to listen.

So every day for three years straight, he offered something small up to her lips. No matter that it hadn't worked the day before, or the day before that, or the day before that. He didn't mind. He just kept talking to her and trying, never losing hope.

Then one day, quite suddenly, she swallowed. Just like that. Down the hatch.

She laughed.

Her dad smiled.

And I cried.

From that day on, she began making rapid progress. Now she sits up in her wheelchair and eats everything by mouth and even feeds herself.

Funny how when we don't see any progress in a person or a situation, we think nothing is happening and probably never will. But stuff is going on that we can't see. God is at work even when it's not readily apparent. And just when we're losing all hope . . . there's suddenly a swallow.

Infuse hope into your girl's heart. Keep trying and keep believing, reminding her—and yourself—that you serve a God of hope.

Fill her head
WITH
life-giving WORDS.

"The voice." Every person has one—that internal message center that speaks nonstop into the mind and heart, informing the "listener" of who she is, what she does, and what others think about her.

In the quiet moments of your daughter's life, what thoughts does she have about herself? What does the voice inside your child's head say?

You are a worthwhile person! or *You are stubborn!*

You are smart! or *You can't do anything right!*

In powerful ways, the messages a child hears repeatedly in childhood become the voice inside her head in adulthood. Words matter.

And that little girl is attentive, even when it seems like she isn't listening. What she hears repeatedly, she will eventually believe about herself. That message— the voice—plays over and over again.

So, what voice will you place in your daughter's head tomorrow through the messages you speak today? Fill her heart and mind with affirming, life-giving words.

BE HER
good friend—
BUT NOT NECESSARILY HER
buddy.

One of my daughters asked me to meet her for coffee recently. She caught me up on all her happenings, and I told her about mine. She made me laugh, as she always does, and we covered lots of ground. Then she told me as I left the café, "Mom, you know you're my best friend, don't you?"

Maybe I did. But it was nice to hear it all the same.

As your daughter grows up, she'll increasingly look to you as not only a parent but also a friend. She's going to want someone to listen to her and to talk about her dreams and ideas with. She'll be glad for your companionship and for fun times together.

But no matter how much fun you have together, she needs you to be her parent more than her pal. In other words, don't let her speak to you or treat you in a manner that suggests you're one of her peers—something I've had to remind our daughters of on occasion. I dearly desire to be their friend but not necessarily their "buddy."

So, while you'll want to pursue a growing friendship with your girl, don't forget she needs you to be her parent even more.

Tell her YOU ARE *proud of her.*

Always be ready with words on your lips for just about anything—from good to great—that your daughter does. Often parents have intense feelings of pride and appreciation for their children, but the kids never know because nothing was said.

Think about this next week or month. Is something coming up that you could highlight in a conversation with your daughter? She needs to know you are deeply proud of her, but she'll never know unless you tell her.

And don't just toss the statement over your shoulder as you are heading to work. Stop, look into her eyes, and tell her from your heart: "I am so proud of you!"

Love her
ENOUGH TO HAVE THE *hard*
conversations.

It's not always easy to be the mom, to say the hard things. So I braced myself for the pushback that was sure to come. My daughter wasn't going to like what I had to say, and I knew it. With one sentence from me, she would feel like her world was coming apart.

In reality, her world would be just fine, but that's not how it would *feel* to her. And those feelings are powerful.

So I braved the emotional storm and said what I knew to be right for her. Her response was exactly what I'd predicted, and it wasn't pretty. At first, she was angry, then came the flood of tears.

Yet I remained unmoved. Not because I'm uncaring. In fact, it's quite the opposite—I love her enough to say the sometimes painful things.

You'll probably have many opportunities over the years to say or do the difficult things. Don't let your daughter's emotions dissuade you. Love her enough to stand strong.

Hike
TOGETHER.

Within a few miles of where you live is a trail or some other park or walk you can take with your daughter. Our family's go-to hike a few miles from our house is Smith Rocks State Park (it's world-famous—you should check it out).

No need for an agenda—just arrange to go and then hit the trail! Without words, you've said to your daughter, "You matter to me" and "I like hanging out with you!" Within no time, your no-agenda hike will turn into a bonding adventure to remember for years to come.

Speak patiently
TO HER.

I hate telling this story. It makes me cringe even now when I think of it.

I'd accompanied our little girl into the public restroom so she wouldn't be in there alone. I was hot and tired, and it had been a long day. She was taking forever to do what she needed to do and—much to my germ-fearing horror—was touching handles and surfaces with her bare hands. So I rushed her along and snapped at her carelessness. I didn't exactly yell at her, but my husband could hear me on the other side of the door.

I know he could hear because he told me so. I was immediately convicted, and my eyes filled with tears—not because of what others might have thought but because of what my dear girl must have thought. Why hadn't I shown more patience? What kind of excuse is "hot" or "tired" when you're talking to someone little whom you love? No excuse.

So, my friend, don't do what I did on that awful hot afternoon in the McDonald's bathroom. Speak patiently to your girl.

MAKE HER *believe* YOU LIKE TO BE *with her.*

You want to be a good parent and give your daughter what she needs—clothes, food, an education, and lessons of various kinds. You pay the bills to keep things in the home and family moving forward. Your efforts are all for her—her well-being, her security.

But there's something she needs far more than the best of what you can provide.

Of course you love her. Of course you'd walk over broken glass on your hands and knees for her. At some deep level, she knows this already—the rock-bottom foundation of your commitment to her. But it's not enough. She needs something more from you.

Your daughter gets a great deal of her self-worth from her relationship with you. Does she consider herself valuable? Does she think she is an interesting person? Does she know you like her company?

She needs to believe, down in her soul, that you genuinely enjoy spending time with her. And not time that is driven by some agenda. For this kind of value message, the trip to soccer practice won't do.

Going somewhere today or tomorrow? To the store? The gas station? Getting takeout? Ask her to come along, and tell her you like being with her because she's a fun, delightful person and you always have a better time when she's along.

It's about being desired, not just being cared for. And just like you do, she needs to feel wanted. Love her by showing her consistently, over time, you like being with her.

Inform her
OF GOD'S
incredible design
FOR HER FEMININE BODY.

Not too long ago, one of my daughters mentioned what I, her mother, said years ago about the beauty—and mystery—of God's design when a woman starts her monthly cycle. I was enthusiastic about how this meant her body was preparing to support a life in her womb someday. Apparently, my daughter never thought about her monthly cycle quite the same after our talk.

And it's true. I genuinely do view it this way, even with its accompanying discomfort and inconvenience. And I hope to communicate to my daughters that periods, sex, pregnancy, labor, and birth are all wonderful miracles, lovingly designed by our good Creator.

While our current culture can take a rather negative view of this incredible process—with an unhealthy emphasis on the "downsides" of being a woman—we want our daughters to see it not as a curse but rather as a reflection of a loving God.

So be sure to bring up the subject if she's approaching womanhood (if you haven't already yet) and enjoy the discussion. Don't consider this topic a onetime conversation; instead, think of it as an ongoing conversation you can have as she continues on into womanhood.

Take a big TRIP together.

Whether it's a few days or a week, at some point set aside space on the schedule to go on a trip with your daughter. Maybe she's graduated from high school or accomplished some other big goal, or maybe you just say, "Road trip!" because you don't need much of a reason. Pick a date and put it on the calendar. It's so simple to do, and it's a big opportunity for the two of you to grow closer.

In a tangible way, your daughter is getting this message: "You are important to me, and I like going places and on adventures with you!" After you've picked the place and date (be sure to seek her input), spend time planning the trip together, which is just another way of saying, "I love you!"

Surprise her
WITH A NO-OCCASION
gift.

As a girl, I'd occasionally come home from school to find a small present waiting for me at the end of my bed. It was never anything expensive or extravagant—just a whimsical gift that told me my mom had been thinking of me.

Usually, she gave me a new book or a pretty scarf or a hair band. I suppose she could have just as easily handed it to me when I walked in the door, but she made it extra special by wrapping it and including a short note too.

I still own most, if not all, of those childhood books with her handwritten notes on the inside pages, and I plan to pass those books down to my own daughters someday.

So think about a sweet gift that would be meaningful to your daughter. This gesture is not about accumulating more "things," but about a thoughtful gift that would delight her heart. Then wrap it up or drop it into a present bag and leave it somewhere she'll be sure to find it. And don't forget to write a little love note too!

Take time out
TO LAUGH
together.

I was right in the middle of a particularly busy day when my daughter came up to show me one of those viral internet videos. Inwardly annoyed, as I hardly had time for such things, I slowed down long enough to watch the two-minute escapade.

Apparently, someone had dressed up in an oversized dinosaur costume and went racing through the neighborhood in a huge storm. And, as silly as it was, how it made me laugh! Ridiculously so, until tears rolled down my face. My daughter found my response even funnier than the video clip. It was two minutes well spent. To this day, she'll send me a GIF or a dinosaur emoji to remind me of that day we laughed until we cried.

If only I'd understood the impact of laughter when our girls were younger. Back then, I took life too seriously and was more focused on all that had to be done. That was before I realized the healing and connection that comes with laughing together.

So stop whatever you're doing right now, because laughter can do more for your relationship than you might realize. Get a little silly or simply focus on the lighter side of life. Watch a romantic comedy or tell knock-knock jokes until you can't see straight.

See if you can get your girl giggling, and then join right in.

Show her HOW TO PREPARE *delicious food.*

My own mother is an excellent cook, and I grew up eating very well. She was into healthy eating long before it was the trend it is now. We always enjoyed fresh, wholesome snacks and sit-down dinners. But, unfortunately, none of these skills (or the interest) were passed down to me. I was too busy doing more "important" things, like studying and traveling.

So when I got married, I had to call my mom and ask her how to make mashed potatoes. I had no idea how they went from a full bag of whole brown potatoes to that creamy white stuff you serve from the bowl. She had to walk me through the process step by step. You can guess that if I didn't know how to make mashed potatoes, then I couldn't make much else either. And you'd be right.

So I made sure my own daughters could cook a variety of dishes. They do not all have the same degree of interest in cooking, but they do consider themselves adequately equipped and can follow just about any recipe.

Cooking is a handy skill to pass down to the ones you love.

Communicate YOUR LOVING *approval.*

Performance-based parenting is one of our most common faults and also one of the most destructive. Your daughter's value comes from being made in the image of God—from being a person He brought into this world. Psalm 139:14 says,

> I will praise You, for I am fearfully and
>   wonderfully made;
> Marvelous are Your works.

To have value, to be loved, she doesn't have to do anything. She's your daughter. There's nothing she has to do to gain your approval. You already approve of her. You love her. She is valuable because she is a creation of God and someone He loves.

Yes, you appreciate your daughter's achievements, but she must never come to believe you love her because of her accomplishments, gifts, looks, or any other thing. Tell her you love her just the way she is. You love *who* she is and her value comes from God, which is something no one can take from her.

Love her BY BEING A PERSON SHE CAN *safely share* HER EMOTIONS WITH.

You should have heard my daughter. Or maybe you shouldn't have, but you probably *could* have if you'd been anywhere nearby. Because that girl was awfully upset, and she was sure letting me know. Loudly. Tearfully. And I started to soften her response.

She stopped me right then and there. "Mom, if I can't tell you how I'm really feeling, who can I tell?" she said.

She had a good point. I want to be that safe person she can come to with her many ups and downs. As a former "stuffer" myself, I know how important it is to avoid stuffing your emotions. In the moment, it may seem like the better, easier response to those strong feelings of anger, fear, or distress, but it will only make things worse over time.

So be that sweet sanctuary for your girl to express her emotions—the good, the bad, and yes, even the ugly.

Take her OUT FOR *ice cream.*

Not far from our home is our favorite ice-cream shop (Italian gelato, actually)—Bonta. It's an artisan specialty shop. They serve signature flavors like Vanilla Bourbon Pecan, Peanut Butter with Theo Fudge, and even Lemon Cream and Candied Ginger. Yes, it's expensive but worth every penny! If you're ever in Bend, Oregon, Bonta is downtown on Bond Street and you'll have to check it out. Our daughters (and my wife, for that matter) are always up for a trip into town for some amazing gelato.

Every town has an ice-cream shop, and there are only four people on the planet who don't like ice cream, so it's an excellent way to enjoy a sweet time with your daughter.

Be her champion
WHEN SHE
stands up
AGAINST THE CROWD.

Our daughter mentioned that she was writing an opinion piece for the school newspaper. She strongly disagreed with the main article on the front page and asked if she could write a counterview. The editor agreed.

One part of me was proud of her willingness to speak up, of course, but another part of me was concerned about the backlash that was sure to come. Seemingly most of her classmates held a different view from her, and the article would not make her very popular on campus. But she wrote it anyway.

Turns out that more people held her view than had vocalized it. Not only that, but her article began a healthy conversation between many people on campus.

While it's never easy to go against the crowd, show your daughter the value of standing up when necessary and holding fast to her views even if it seems like no one else shares them.

Our world needs this kind of conviction. Not only that, you never know what important conversations might result from your daughter's courage. Champion your girl as she takes a stand.

TELL YOUR DAUGHTER, *"I will provide for you."*

Part of your daughter's sense of security comes from knowing she doesn't have to worry where the next peanut butter sandwich is coming from. You are her provider. Certainly, this world will do its best to obscure the difference between legitimate needs and wants, and it's important to provide perspective, but providing is your job.

The Bible (both the Old and New Testaments) is surprisingly harsh on the one who doesn't provide for their family's basic needs. First Timothy 5:8 says, "But if any provide not for his own, and specially for those of his own house, he hath denied the faith, and is worse than an infidel" (KJV).

Gently help your daughter understand the difference between needs and wants, but strongly affirm that you will be there to provide for her.

LET YOUR DAUGHTER *know* YOU'LL ALWAYS BE *by her side.*

That mother-daughter relationship isn't as easy as one might think. I used to believe it would come naturally somehow. Why wouldn't it? We come from the same family, and I've obviously known her for her entire life. We have so much in common.

But then the differences between me and one of my daughters were greater than I had first guessed. And it's tempting to "give up" when things get tough and the gap seems too wide.

But I'm glad—so very, very glad—we both hung in there, because now that girl and I have grown into good friends. But it's less because we're so much alike than it is because we've chosen love.

And if you happen to be in the "wide gap" season with your daughter right now? Don't give up. She needs you to stay with her . . . more than she might say or even know. Tell her you love her and you're not going anywhere.

She will always be your girl.

Bake a batch
OF HOMEMADE COOKIES
together.

If you're the kind of parent who does everything "for" rather than "with" your daughter, back off, slow down, and do something together! And if you've never baked, you can do it! It's not that hard (just follow a recipe), and it will be a fun, memorable experience you can share.

Try out a new chocolate chip cookie recipe or maybe your mother's old-fashioned gingersnaps. You can hardly go wrong with a fresh batch of homemade cookies!

Pursue
HER HEART
more than
HER GOOD BEHAVIOR.

Our third daughter and I weren't always as close as we are now. And as her mother, I can't tell you how sorry I am that I didn't recognize the distance earlier. My focus was on making it through the day and getting her to the correct place on time rather than seeing her heart and what she needed from me.

I thought I was doing the right thing by making sure she did her chores and her schoolwork—and there's a place for that—but her well-being and our relationship should have been my first concern. And a child knows the difference.

It's funny how we, as parents, can get caught up in the things that don't matter that much. We're tempted to fixate on a clean house and well-behaved kids. Or the checklist and the good life.

When, in reality, our relationships should take priority.

You might be tempted to consider that difficult or strong-willed child and think, *If I can only get her to behave, then later we can enjoy that kind of sweetness,* when it's actually the other way around.

You have a sweet relationship, and from that foundation you can train and teach your child.

So don't wait for "closeness" to fall into place. Pursue her heart now.

Give YOUR DAUGHTER *new responsibility.*

There is nothing like trusting your daughter with a new responsibility to bring out a sense of healthy pride in who she is and how she sees herself.

When you give her a task or assignment, you are essentially informing her of how highly you think of her. She will think, *I am a person worthy of being trusted. I am a person who can do extraordinary things. I have a significant contribution to make. My parents believe in me!*

Depending on your daughter's age, the tasks you give her will vary greatly. Even if she's a toddler, you can begin by trusting her to carry her cup to the sink (and be sure to praise her to the sky when she is successful!).

Most daughters are capable of far more than many parents think. When you trust her and prove that you believe in her ability to accomplish something important, you will grow closer to her and her self-confidence will increase.

Encourage CONFIDENCE IN *her appearance.*

"Do you think I'm pretty, Mom?"

I couldn't believe she would ask such a question. Not because I'm her mom, but because she even felt the need to ask. And I have to say, it was a bit of a wake-up call. I had underestimated the influence of social media and famous celebrities on her dear, young life.

I thought she would see that she's lovely simply by looking in the mirror. I didn't yet realize how much today's (false) standard of beauty can mess with a girl's mind.

We want our daughters to be aware of beauty—to feel beautiful—but not get lost in the chase. We don't want them to be searching for some elusive, deceptive image of beauty or seeking a kind of "pretty" that doesn't exist outside of Photoshop and plastic surgery. Doing so would be a terrible waste of their time, energy, and gifts.

No, we want our daughters to recognize—and embrace—that true beauty comes from being made in God's image.

Assure her
OF YOUR *protection*.

When our daughters were young teenagers, we had a person in our lives who, looking back, we now are certain had borderline personality disorder. As their dad, I wish I'd had clarity at the time, because this person was beyond awful and very destructive. I should have severed the relationship entirely after the first offense. I didn't, and it was a bad parenting mistake that damaged my daughters' sense of being protected.

They've forgiven me now, but oh, how I wish I had those years to do over.

We never know what life will throw at us. We never know how we may be threatened in big or small ways. We never know how people will attempt to take advantage of us. This world can be threatening, scary, and intimidating for your daughter. She needs to know you are watching over her. She needs to understand you will stand beside her, and if need be, you will take the incoming hit. Wherever it may be coming from.

By all means, tell her you will protect her—then make sure you follow through, again and again.

GO TO A *concert* OR *performance* TOGETHER.

When I was a young girl, my dad took me to a concert at Knott's Berry Farm in Southern California. I don't know if it was his idea or my mom's, but it was dazzling and one of my favorite childhood memories. I was mesmerized by the large crowd, bright lights, and incredible talent, and my young heart was moved deeply by the music.

To be honest, the event was a bit outside both our comfort zones, a stretch for us both. But it was a risk worth taking and an evening I'll never forget.

When your daughter is old enough, start looking for an event you think she'll enjoy and book a night out. Make a memory of a lifetime together.

Praise her
FOR A JOB
well done.

It's easy to give your daughter a task and then forget all about the assignment. Life moves forward with the speed and force of a fighter jet. Who has time to look back and reflect positively on the day, week, or month? But a wise parent won't let a job completed well pass without recognizing the excellent work that was done.

"I really appreciate when you . . ."

"Thanks so much for completing that . . ."

"You really did a great job with . . ."

Sometimes the easiest things are the things we most easily pass over. But this is a huge mistake.

What adult doesn't deeply appreciate being recognized and praised in the workplace when they accomplish an assigned task? The truth is, we all *love* praise and recognition!

To become her best, your daughter needs to hear the love, appreciation, and pleasure in your voice as you praise her excellent work, whatever it may be. She needs to see the approval on your face—your countenance.

You have at your disposal genuine power to bring positive reinforcement to your daughter's heart. Your approval and encouragement can have a strong impact on her life and perspective.

THROW A *party* WITH OR FOR *her.*

Our daughter said she wanted to throw a "murder mystery" party. I'd never heard of such a crazy event before, but I had to admit that it did sound interesting. So she put together the necessary pieces and sent out the invitations. The only thing left for her dad and me to do was dress up and follow the script. He was designated the "head butler," and I was the "housemaid." It turned out to be more fun than we had anticipated (and I don't just mean for the kids).

The best part was that we didn't throw this party for anyone's birthday either. It was simply a night to remember.

So don't necessarily wait for a special occasion. Pull out the calendar and pick a date that would be perfect for a no-good-reason party. And then watch your daughter shine.

Give her
A VISION FOR THE
woman
SHE IS
becoming.

Your daughter is becoming a woman. It's the natural course of life as the years pass. The question is, What kind of woman is she becoming? She wonders this herself, perhaps not in those exact words, but the thought of who she will be when she is an adult is on her mind from time to time as she matures.

Right now, today, you can speak into her mind and heart a truth that will profoundly impact her future. The choices she makes today are building something. Together they are forming the life she will have on every level. The kind of person she will be is in the making right now. Her tomorrow is nothing more than the culmination of the decisions she is making today.

Love your daughter by giving her a vision of the woman she is becoming. Speak to her the truth of God's best for her—a life that draws her closer to Him and His ways every day. Teach her that she is not a passive bystander to her own life; she is, in fact, building her future. It's an empowering truth for a young girl who is growing into a woman.

CONSIDER
getting healthy
TOGETHER.

I'd been going to an exercise studio for a while when I asked one of my daughters if she'd be up for working out with her mom.

At first, she said she wasn't interested. But I asked again after some time had gone by. Eventually, she agreed to give it a go. Now we have the best time working out at the same studio. We exercise, we laugh, and we sweat. And going together has turned exercising into something fun for both of us.

So maybe working out isn't your thing, but if you're at all open to it, ask your girl if she'd like to try a workout with you. Try running, cycling, going to the gym, dancing, skating, or swimming.

Enjoy growing stronger side by side.

Arrange FOR A *picnic* IN THE *park.*

It may sound like a logistics challenge, but nothing could be easier than having a picnic in the park. We're not talking about a scene out of a Jane Austen novel. All you have to do is go to the market, get a couple of sandwiches, drinks, fruit, and perhaps some special chocolate. Then bring a blanket from home, and you're all set to go.

You might also want to pack a book to read or a Frisbee to toss around. Or maybe you'll just want to lay on the grass and look at the clouds in the sky.

Take her for a picnic and see how quickly it becomes a favorite outing for you both.

Take note
OF WHAT BOTHERS
your daughter
AND THEN *stop* DOING IT.

It's funny how unaware a mother can be. I was clueless when my daughter first told me how much this one thing bugged her. Oblivious, I didn't even know what she meant. But apparently, when I give her a hug, after a few seconds or so, I softly start patting her back. She told me it was my way of telling her, "Okay, time to run along now."

I had no idea that I did this or what it was communicating to her. But she's right, as I can see myself unconsciously getting restless and ready to get on with other things while we're still in the middle of what was supposed to be a warm hug.

I'm glad she told me, however, and I'm working hard to stop this annoying habit. It's made me more aware of other things I do that cause her unnecessary irritation.

So, start observing those behaviors or words that rub your girl the wrong way. You might even want to ask her outright what annoys her! Then stop doing it.

Be gentle WITH HER *mistakes.*

Mistakes are guaranteed; your daughter is going to mess up. How do you handle those moments?

People make errors for dozens of reasons: wrong information, carelessness, inability to complete a given task, a bad judgment call. Mistakes are one of God's ways of teaching and maturing us, but we completely miss this opportunity to change when we overreact, condemn, respond in anger, ridicule, or make a joke out of the moment. I, Matt, know a woman who was paranoid every time she went into the kitchen to make dinner because of the ridicule she regularly received for her misguided efforts when she was growing up.

When you respond in these sinful ways (that's what it is—*sin*), all the positive benefits of the experience evaporate. Every moment polluted with anger, ridicule, or sarcasm destroys your relationship with your daughter.

While I've never ridiculed my children or treated their errors with sarcasm, I have chosen to sin in anger (never forget, anger is a sinful choice—every time) in response to our daughters' mistakes. I have had to humble myself before each one, name my sin, and ask for forgiveness (yes, I cried).

In my case, the irony is that my fleshly anger rears its head in response to not the big things but the small things. If my daughter drove our car into the front living room, I wouldn't flinch. I take the big stuff in stride. But leave a loaf of mom's freshly baked bread on the counter after you've helped yourself and expect someone else to pick up the mess—steam comes out my ears. It's sinful. It's destructive.

Have you forgotten the many mistakes you've made? Have you reacted with harshness when gentleness was needed? In the moment, it's easy to do. But it's a healthy exercise to reflect on the dozens (and dozens and dozens!) of blunders you've made. When you're honest with yourself, you'll have far more grace for your daughter. Most mistakes could happen to anyone.

When you approach her mistakes with gentleness, it's like carefully opening the door of your daughter's heart. God can then use that moment the way He intended—for learning, growing, and maturing.

Set aside A SPECIFIC *time* TO *focus on her*.

"Mom, I wish you spent more time with me."

I couldn't believe what I was hearing from my daughter's mouth. Before she said that, I would have told you I spent tons of time with her. As a stay-at-home mom, I was with our girls for most of the day. But it turns out that there's a big difference between being around your daughter, doing all those normal, daily kinds of things, and actually setting aside a designated time intended specifically for only you and her.

And that's what my daughter was trying to tell me that day. She didn't merely want to be around me (although there's a benefit to that as well), she wanted me to give her my full attention. No, better than that, she wanted that time to be about her and me *together*.

Don't wait for your daughter to ask; start planning something special for you to do together. It doesn't have to be fancy: plan a tea for two, set up a board game, or go into town together.

Teach her
THE PROPER
value of money.

Teaching your daughter the value of money is a tangible, practical way to show love to her. Part of your job is to prepare her for the realities of the world she will encounter when she is on her own. Perhaps she'll get married. Maybe she won't. Perhaps she'll receive some kind of family inheritance when she leaves the house. Maybe she won't. Whatever she encounters in life, will she be able to look after herself?

Perhaps start by letting her purchase the groceries each week for a given time. Then let her (under supervision, of course) pay the electric/gas bill and the mortgage either online or by writing a check. Let her see what it takes to keep your household running. Then, at some point, give her a budget for her clothes for the coming year, but remember that discussion about being gentle with her mistakes!

While managing finances is a practical and necessary skill, there is an aspect of money that, for the Christian, is more important than all the rest. Don't neglect to teach your daughter that money is entrusted to her by God. The Bible warns that money can easily become an idol—something we covet and seek to acquire, something we worship. The love of money is the root of all kinds of evil (1 Tim. 6:10). Those who desire to be rich pierce themselves through with many sorrows (1 Tim. 6:10). And, finally, you can't serve both God and money (Matt. 6:24). If we love money, we've already chosen our god.

Offer your daughter God's perspective on money. Teach her the proper value of money.

Be interested
IN HER *interests.*

If I remember correctly, it all started with cupcakes. My daughter loved baking them, serving them, and celebrating with them. Then somehow those pink, fluffy cupcakes grew into rather elaborate tea parties for young girls—"Little Princess Tea Parties"—and they were a huge success.

Not everyone enjoys hosting dozens of little princess girls licking sticky cupcakes and sipping tea in their living room. Personally, I liked the idea of it better than the reality. But my daughter thrived in this environment. She loved every minute of it—the planning, the execution, and the actual event. She didn't even mind the cleanup!

Although they were a bit of a stretch for me, a busy mom and committed introvert, I could see her come to life at these tea parties. So it was an opportunity to put aside my own preferences and show genuine excitement for the things she treasured.

Show enthusiasm and support for all her unique interests.

Encourage her
TO VALUE THE VIEWS
of others.

When we respect other people, they are far more ready to return the honor. This is an invaluable life skill that will enrich your daughter's character. The principal way of respecting another person is to be authentically interested in what they have to say and think. Help your daughter understand and make the connection between the two.

Valuing someone's opinion doesn't mean you must embrace it, but it's always important to carefully listen.

Move in close
IF SHE FEELS *far away*.

Our young adult daughter texted me this yesterday: "Hey, how about I stop by and bring you a coffee, Mom? If you have the time?"

Oh my. YES!

And maybe you're thinking how easy it must be for her and me. How natural that she'd stop by on a Saturday afternoon and bring me a coffee and want to talk. It might be natural now, but it wasn't always like that. I first noticed the distance when she was about four years old. I could give you good reasons for it, but it doesn't matter so much why as it does that her heart was far from mine.

So I committed the next year to that dear girl. I more or less glued her to my side. We did everything together—errands, chores, etc. And I held my breath, wondering if reattachment between parent and child was a thing.

Thankfully, our season of being inseparable seemed to work. Maybe you have no idea what I'm talking about. But if you have a child who seems far away from you, don't let go.

Lean in, and don't stop reaching for her until you're close again.

Show her
THE WISDOM IN
walking humbly.

The person who is shown to be wrong and won't change damages every relationship they have. It's bad enough that a sibling, friend, coworker, husband, or wife relationship is wounded because of the sin of pride (why else does a person stubbornly refuse to change in the face of incontrovertible facts?), but the relational damage goes far beyond these temporal relationships. In fact, it goes all the way to heaven.

First Peter 5:5 says,

> God resists the proud,
> But gives grace to the humble.

Your daughter doesn't want, and certainly doesn't need, God to oppose her. Teach her that the only impediment to being willing to change when she is wrong is pride, which God hates.

Don't try to teach her in real time, during some emotionally intense altercation. Take up the conversation about humility apart from the incident, when cooler thinking prevails.

Walk humbly and encourage her to do the same.

GIVE HER
grace
IN *growing up.*

Just when I'm convinced my daughter has "got it" and reached a new stage of maturity, she will say or do something that will make me question what I was thinking. And I'm tempted to despair and wonder if she's going to stay girlish forever. Then the very next day she will shock me with an older-than-her-years insight or unusually mature decision.

You probably want your daughter to grow up at a steady incline, when in reality, it's more of a roller-coaster ride.

She's not always going to get things right, and that's okay. Keep telling yourself that how it is today isn't how it's always going to be. Your daughter will learn and grow, but you have to give her the necessary time and space to do so.

And when you find yourself frustrated? Look back at your own childhood and recall when you were that age and how much you wished your parents would have been patient and understanding with you. Then think about how you can offer that kind of patient grace to your daughter.

Growing up is a process, so show some patience. She needs it.

Dress up
AND TAKE HER TO
dinner.

In Central Oregon, where we live, dressing up often means putting on a new pair of jeans! Even if your daughter is not into fashion, you two can still dress up for an evening out on the town. Wherever you live, there's likely a restaurant where she would love to have dinner with you.

She'll need a little notice, so propose the idea a few days in advance. To get the conversation started once the meal begins, ask her about her life, what she's thinking about, what she's concerned with, what she's been doing lately.

When was the last time you took your daughter out? Don't let this week pass without inviting her out and making all the arrangements.

Value her
THOUGHTS AND PERSPECTIVE.

I, Lisa, asked one young friend what said love to her, although I had already guessed what her answer would be. But I was wrong. She replied with something I never would have considered.

She shared that she feels loved and valued when her parents ask her views. Her family had recently had to make a momentous decision, and they had wanted to hear her perspective on the situation. This invitation communicated to her that she was important and her views mattered. It said love to her.

As a parent, we can be overly concerned with filling our daughter's head with everything we think she should know and understand. We offer our views and inform her of our way of looking at things.

We can get so wrapped up in pouring out our own thoughts that we neglect to ask her about hers. "What do you think of that?" "What would you do in that situation?" "What's your opinion on that topic?" When she's given the chance, you might be surprised how well she thinks and how much she has to offer. Not only will you learn more about what's on her mind, but she will also feel respected and loved by your interest in her thoughts.

So find out what she's thinking and let her know you care deeply about her perspective.

TAKE A MEAL TO
someone in need.

Start by asking your daughter if she knows of someone who might be in need of a meal. Maybe it's someone who is in the middle of a move or who has found themselves in hard times. The two of you can brainstorm who might welcome the gift of a dinner from you both.

In our church community, we have many opportunities to bless families with a meal. As soon as a baby is born or someone gets sick, the meal train is established. In just about any church community or nearby neighborhood, there will be a need, at some point, to provide a dinner.

Jump at the chance. It's a beautiful thing to prepare your best dish to bless someone else.

Plan and cook the meal with your daughter. It's crucial that she genuinely contributes to the endeavor. She'll feel valued by you and enjoy the process of giving much more.

CALM HER
fears AND *anxieties.*

When our daughter was young, she was brave in so many ways, but she hated it when her dad and I traveled out of town. As soon as we would announce an upcoming trip, she'd start to spiral downward. We'd do what we could to reassure her that she'd be fine and that we were coming back. A trusted friend would even stay with her, and she wouldn't be alone.

But the mere thought of us being away for a single night sent her into a tearful panic.

Part of me wanted to tell her to get a grip, while the other part had compassion for her fears. I racked my brain trying to think of what I could do to help her while we were gone. Then I remembered her sensitivity to scent and touch, and the idea came to me: I'd let her sleep in my robe and use my pillow. It might not be me, but it would smell and feel like me.

And this turned out to be a significant comfort to her when we traveled.

So, rather than dismiss your daughter's fears—or wish she'd just get a grip—do what you can to calm her anxieties and let her know how deeply you care.

HEAD OUT TO A
farmers market
TOGETHER.

Just about every large and small town has a farmers market. It's a great outing in the summer or fall. And, with the two of you, there can be only one purpose—to be together. That's it. You can wander through the booths and check out the crafts together and then explore the many great options for lunch. Enjoy the gorgeous selection of homegrown produce and taste the samples of homemade jams.

If you're the type who doesn't like shopping, remind yourself that this trip has nothing to do with shopping. It's about "being." Remember, strolling slowly with your daughter is saying love to her.

Learn YOUR DAUGHTER'S *love language* AND SPEAK IT *often.*

What says love to your girl? Study her closely and notice what kinds of things fill her heart.

Ask her directly if she's old enough to know and tell you. Does she appreciate quality time? Or maybe words of affirmation? Receiving gifts? Acts of service? Physical touch? All these things have a place in a close relationship, but some speak louder than others, and it's worth considering what speaks loudest to your daughter.

Sometimes you might feel like you are doing all you can to show love to her, only to find out that it doesn't mean as much to her as you thought it would. That's because it's not her love language. Once you know what kinds of things make her feel loved, then you can focus on those that say love the most to her.

SHOW YOUR DAUGHTER HOW TO
work hard
AND
cheerfully.

A willingness to work hard and cheerfully is a great gift every parent should give to their daughter. It is one of those gifts, however, that is given only by example. Do you work hard and happily? Your daughter is watching and taking mental notes. If you neglect your work or do it with complaining, eye rolls, and tired, dissatisfied sighs, she will not receive your vital gift toward her bright future.

Love your daughter by giving her a deep sense of balanced self-respect that comes only through knowing how to work hard—and enjoying it. A daughter who has learned the value and blessing of working cheerfully will be successful anywhere she lives and will lead a happier life.

Help YOUR DAUGHTER DEVELOP *healthy friendships.*

I'm a big fan of friendship. And I believe good friendships are an important—and necessary—part of a person's life. We were never meant to be loners. God intended for us to love and walk with others. I get that.

But here's something I didn't really "get" until the last few years: friendship is a skill that can be learned and pursued.

I wish I would have understood that better when I was a young girl. I think it would have helped me in my relationships with other girls. I guess I thought friendship just kind of happened—you know, either it worked or it didn't work.

Let's teach our daughters differently. Let's help them understand what it means to find a friend and how to be a good friend. How to look for qualities such as honesty, loyalty, and kindness.

Help your daughter develop valuable friendships with other like-minded girls.

TEACH HER TO
respect herself.

At some point, your daughter will encounter people who will treat her with disrespect. It's just the way of this sinful world. The time will come when she will have to stand up for herself. She's going to need inner strength, a certain toughness of spirit.

If your daughter is young, defend her and make her feel your protection. As she grows older and more aware, teach her to respect herself and maintain her poise when tough moments arrive. She doesn't have to meet insult with insult. She doesn't need to deliver a harsh, sarcastic response.

Teach your daughter to ignore most disrespect—to rise above it and move on. She has better things to do than care about and respond to comments from people who choose to act small. Returning kindness when it isn't deserved is God's way, and it speaks deeply to the settled inner strength of anyone who responds this way.

In reaction to the disrespect that must not be ignored, she can be gracious, calm, and as tough as nails. Your daughter's strength of mind comes from knowing who she is in Christ, knowing she is of immense value, and knowing you have her back.

Never, ever
GIVE UP ON
her.

"Oh, I give up!"

I never intended to say it aloud, but I was extremely frustrated with one of my daughters and it slipped out. Not a great thing for a mother to say, I admit. And I certainly didn't mean for her to hear it, as I was talking more to myself than to her.

But she did hear it. And I hurt her badly.

She told me later that day, with tears in her eyes, "Please don't ever give up on me. Even if everyone else in the world does, I can't have you giving up. Please. I don't know if I'll make it if you do."

This was a life-changing moment in my parenting. How could I not have realized the power that I had in her young life? I promised myself that day that I'd never again say those words, or even allow those thoughts, in regard to my daughter.

Don't make my same mistake. Never, ever give up on your girl.

Frame AND *display* A PICTURE OF THE *two of you.*

In my office, you'll immediately spot several framed pictures of me with one or another of my girls. One is of me in a suit and tie and my daughter in a full-length red gown at a flute concert that she starred in. Another is me with our special-needs daughter laughing with delight from her wheelchair. I love looking up at these beautiful girls and enjoying those memories in the middle of my workday. And I especially love it when they come in and I see the joy on their faces too.

Pick a setting, get some pictures of the two of you, then get one framed and give her a copy. Be sure to display your copy in a prominent place in your home or office. Show the world—but most of all her—that she's special and you treasure the times you enjoy with her.

TAKE A MOMENT TO
enjoy
A CUP OF TEA *together.*

Or coffee or juice or cola or whatever she chooses.

Although as a mother of eight children I ran a busy household, on most days my daughters and I would sit down and "take tea" together for twenty to thirty minutes (it's possible we watched *Pride & Prejudice* one too many times). While this ritual started out as one of those "just for fun" things, it turned into a time that we girls looked forward to in the afternoon. With everyone going in so many different directions, our afternoon tea became a sweet time for us to be together.

So often we think we don't have time or are too distracted to consider taking a break like this in the middle of our days. But this break turned into a critical time of connection, especially when the girls got into their teenage years and we had those tricky, growing-up topics to work through together. Talking about growing into womanhood over a cup of tea made for a lovely afternoon break.

Welcome HER *questions*
ON SEXUAL TOPICS.

Here's an area I wish I would have handled better with our girls. I wasn't super comfortable talking about sexual things, so I unconsciously avoided the topics as much as possible—as if silence would somehow make them go away. Lame, I know.

This hesitant approach left my daughters to their own devices. And although information is out there, especially on the internet (far too much, in my opinion), it's not where you'd want your girls to turn. The best way for your daughter to seek answers is in the safety of her relationship with you, her mom.

Let her know you're available to answer her questions, no matter how awkward or personal they may be. And reassure her that you will listen without judgment—although this might be harder than it sounds. Pretend, if you have to. Because if you don't talk to her about such things, someone else will.

Welcome your girl's sexual questions out of love and care for her.

EMBRACE HER *transition* TO *womanhood*.

Last week I was invited to a special celebration for the daughter of good friends of ours. The celebration was not for her birthday or a specific holiday but to celebrate the beginning of her journey into womanhood. The family asked a handful of women who know this girl well to speak words of wisdom, encouragement, and hope into her life as she moves toward maturity.

Several of us women talked about the event afterward and how such things aren't celebrated anymore. We have forgotten the power of acknowledging a new season and the beauty in it too.

Something in us wants our daughters to stay little girls forever. Maybe we don't like change or perhaps we want her to avoid the ups and downs of womanhood. But rather than denying that your daughter is growing up, embrace the process. She needs you to walk through it with her rather than fight against it.

So tell her you're excited about what's coming and how she's maturing. Embrace the transition and encourage her to embrace it as well. You might even consider celebrating it with a special event with close friends and family!

Tell her,
"YOU ARE BEAUTIFUL."

Even if a young girl is, by all standards, a total knockout, this world will do its best to convince her of the opposite. Just about every voice in your daughter's world will tell her that she is anything but beautiful. Advertisers want her to feel inadequate so she will desire their clothes, makeup, hair products, etc. The last thing your daughter will hear from most encounters she has with twenty-first-century culture is that she is beautiful and great just the way she is, that she meets the expectations placed on her.

This is why your voice is critical. You stand like a guardian over her against a culture that desires to twist her perception of herself to its will. Don't let that happen. She needs to hear regularly that she is, indeed, lovely—inside and out. Love her today by telling her, "You are beautiful!"

Believe
YOUR DAUGHTER IS AN
overcomer.

If you met her, you wouldn't think our third daughter could've been a professional thief. Maybe she doesn't look like that now, but we sure worried about it when she was a sneaking-in-the-pantry, stealing-candy-out-of-the-jar three-year-old.

I could already picture her life on the run. Her future years in the penitentiary. As her parent, I nearly despaired. I wondered where we had gone wrong. My daughter and I laugh about it now, but it wasn't so funny back then, I can tell you.

So I have compassion when I hear another parent worry about their daughter's behavior. How this daughter screams or throws things at the other kids. How she hits or doesn't play nicely with her siblings. And such things definitely need to be addressed, worked on, corrected.

But you know what else? Your daughter needs you, the parent, to speak life-giving truth and to speak it to her and the people around you both. She needs to know you believe she is going to conquer her weaknesses and obstacles. Communicate that no matter what her challenges or mistakes may be, she is an overcomer.

VOLUNTEER
together.

There's always something you can volunteer to do. Benevolent organizations need the help of volunteers all the time. You can also offer friends or family simple acts of kindness.

Not long ago, my friend Aaron Smith called us up and said, "How about we come over and weed your flower beds" (we have a lot of them!). Before long, he and Jennifer and their beautiful family were here at our home, helping until the job was done. We were super blessed! Perhaps you know someone who could use some help with their flower beds?

Start searching out opportunities to help those in your church, community, or city, and then volunteer with your daughter to meet those needs.

Listen TO YOUR DAUGHTER'S DREAMS—NO MATTER *how crazy!*

Two days after her college graduation, our second daughter took off for a month in Uganda. She went to give a hand to a friend who cares for quite a few orphans and children with special needs. Although this adventure might have seemed sudden or surprising to some, it wasn't to us. We had heard about this dream—and seen it in her eyes—ever since she was a young girl.

Listen to your girl dream, and understand that some girls are more dramatic dreamers than others. If she comes to you with one dream after another, each one bigger than the last? Be willing to listen. More than that, listen with enthusiasm and only later, if needed, add a little tempering wisdom when appropriate.

You never know where a dream is going to take her. Don't you want to be the one by her side when it leads to something spectacular?

Encourage HER MANY *gifts.*

Have you thought about your daughter's unique gifts? These special God-given abilities can often be seen at a very early age. Are you looking for them? Do you know what your daughter's gifts are right now? And more important, does your daughter know that you recognize what they are?

Remind your daughter today that you see her unique strengths, skills, and abilities and that you really admire them. Remind her that they are from God for her to bless the people and world around her. She has a special purpose in this world in God's plan, and her gifts are a big part of that.

Many parents make the mistake of wanting their daughters to love what they love—to be interested in the things they are interested in. Despite it being a terrible parenting mistake, many parents attempt to live vicariously through their children. A wise parent seeks opportunities for their daughter's gifts to develop.

Get to know her gifts and make their development a priority in your weekly schedule.

Seek HER *out.*

My girls recently mentioned how much they appreciate being checked on by their mom. They like it when I pop in to see how they're doing. As they're rather independent-minded, this took me by surprise. But they explained that it's nice to know that I care enough to look for them, to ask about what they're up to and how they're feeling about life—not in a nosy, controlling way, but because I care how they're doing.

Don't wait for your daughter to come to you. She longs to be pursued. She wants you to be interested in her and to know you are caring for her. Seek her out.

USE A *kind tone* WHEN *speaking* WITH HER.

You may not have meant to speak to her with an edge, but there it was . . . again. We often take the most liberties with the people we love the most. You would rarely, if ever, speak to your neighbor's daughter with a hard edge in your voice. Doesn't your daughter deserve the same?

The way you speak to her is just as crucial as what you actually say. When you use a kind tone, you're enabling your daughter to hear what you're trying to say. You're also providing an example of how she should interact with others.

Harshness closes her heart, but a kind tone opens it.

LOOK FOR *music* TO *enjoy together.*

Our daughter said she was studying in a café when a certain classical piece came over the speakers that reminded her of her mom. She knew how much I liked this song, and we'd listened to it dozens of times when she was growing up.

So she called to say she was thinking of me and held the phone up so I could hear the familiar tune. We were both taken back to a time when we lived close and loved some of the same things. And that song was one of them. Now she was at school three thousand miles away, and hearing this one song made us feel like we were once again together in the same room, even if only for a few minutes.

So don't underestimate the power of music. Introduce her to the kinds of music you admire and be willing to give hers a try as well, especially as she gets older. You might discover a new genre that you've not appreciated before.

Then the next thing you know, she'll be calling you in the middle of the day from thousands of miles away, and all because of one favorite song. Share the beauty of music together.

ENJOY *her unique* PERSONALITY *differences.*

At times, it can be challenging not to chafe at the personality differences of others. After all, our way is the "right way"! As time passes, many parents reconcile themselves to "putting up with" their daughters' different personalities. No more friction. That's good. Or so it seems. But in reality, this is so much less than what we can—and should—enjoy.

As her parent, you can choose, right now, to appreciate your daughter's unique personality. You can decide that instead of enduring her differences with low-grade or hidden disapproval, you are going to embrace and celebrate them. You can decide to enjoy her "otherness."

When you are frustrated with or disapprove of her personality, you are actually telling your daughter something is wrong with her—that she doesn't quite measure up somehow. So harmful, so unnecessary, and so very wrong and destructive.

Choose to like how God made her, with all her personality differences. Doing so is another meaningful way to love this unique creation of God, your daughter.

Help HER *be flexible.*

As I happen to be a naturally enthusiastic planner myself, I had to learn the hard way the importance of flexibility. I'd set my heart on a plan, then when things didn't go the way they were supposed to, I'd be devastated.

And I spent way too much of my earlier life being devastated.

Now one of my daughters is the ultimate planner, and she, too, struggles with being flexible. She has a lot of strong qualities, but "going with the flow" is not one of them. Yet we can control only so much in this world and sometimes—maybe even often—things don't go according to plan.

Don't allow your daughter to let a change of plans ruin her day; instead, help her see that it's okay and she has the chance to adjust and accept the new situation.

Learning to go with the flow now will help her so much in the years ahead.

Buy HER FAVORITE *chocolate.*

The next time you're in the store, pick up your daughter's favorite chocolate (or something you know she'll love) and leave it in her room, perhaps including a note that says, "Just thought of you!" or something similar.

It's easy to forget that a small, simple gesture can have such power. It says you are thinking of her, and she will love to know that she was on your mind.

Guide her WITH *wise instruction.*

The phone rang late one night, and it was one of my daughters calling from college. She was in a relational dilemma and wanted to know what she should do. Should she say something to her friend? Or should she stay silent? The situation was complicated and would have a cost either way she went.

She called to see what I'd advise as her mother.

I did my best to offer what insight I could and told her I'd pray for wisdom for her too. But I couldn't help but be grateful that as a young adult, she'd turned to me—and not only her peers—for counsel.

But the relationship between the two of us that led her to make that phone call? It didn't start that night. That relationship began much earlier, when she was a little girl. Those hours of sitting on the edge of her bed, talking through moral dilemmas and challenging choices, added up over the years.

So don't hesitate to offer your knowledge and experience to your daughter. She needs you to help her sort through the choices, relationships, struggles, and challenges she faces as a young woman. Your wisdom is a loving gift to her.

Invite her
INTO YOUR WORLD.

Providing for your family is a direct responsibility given to you by God. But if you're not careful, you might think providing for your daughter is the same as welcoming her into your world. Many girls lead physically close but emotionally distant lives from their parents, but that's not your daughter's fault.

Does your daughter know anything about your work? Does she know how to cook like you do? Does she know how you organize your priorities? Does she know about how you give a portion of your money to the local church and to other charities? Does she know what you care deeply about? Does she know what you value in close relationships with others?

Inviting your daughter into your world is as simple as sharing your life with her—what you do and why you do it. Her age will dictate what details you can share, but bringing her into your world will give her a growing understanding of and respect for you as her dad/mom. It will also bring you closer in your relationship.

Cook
A GOURMET MEAL
together.

What do you get for the man who has everything? Or at least for the guy who doesn't want much?

It was Matt's birthday, and that was the question my daughter and I were pondering. After some discussion, we decided that rather than getting him a "thing" he likely didn't need or even want, we'd make him a fancy meal instead.

I don't think I had ever seen this side of our daughter before that event. Once we got going, she proved she has amazing talent and creativity when it comes to preparing a meal. Yes, it was an unexpected and delicious surprise for her dad, but better than that, it was a bonding time for us both. A wonderful present for him but a lovely gift to us all.

So you never know, why not see what the two of you can cook up together?

Show her
HOW MUCH
God loves her.

The Bible is the record of what God is doing in this world. It's also the record of His love for each one of us. Take some time to search out a few verses from the Bible that convey God's love for your daughter.

If you don't know where to begin, read 1 John. There are also these beautiful verses found in Psalm 139:

> For You formed my inward parts;
> You covered me in my mother's womb.
> I will praise You, for I am fearfully and
>   wonderfully made;
> Marvelous are Your works,
> And that my soul knows very well.
> My frame was not hidden from You,
> When I was made in secret,
> And skillfully wrought in the lowest parts of the
>   earth.
> Your eyes saw my substance, being yet unformed.
> And in Your book they all were written,
> The days fashioned for me,
> When as yet there were none of them.

How precious also are Your thoughts to me, O
    God!
How great is the sum of them!
If I should count them, they would be more in
    number than the sand;
When I awake, I am still with You. (vv. 13–18)

Read them to your daughter (in fact, read the entire chapter—it's not too long!), and impress upon her God's lasting, immovable love for her.

TAKE HER *somewhere special* FOR AN *overnight.*

With so many kids and a tight budget, we never found it easy to "slip away" with only one child, but doing so turned out to be a far greater investment than I could have known at the time. We started this tradition when our oldest daughter was eleven, and it became such a memorable time that we began doing it with each of our girls as we were able—which wasn't often.

The trip doesn't have to be far away or extravagant, just make sure it's only the two of you and someplace away from home.

Plan a few fun things. Maybe dress up and go out to eat or stay in the hotel room and watch an old classic movie in your pajamas. Talk, laugh, and give her your undivided attention. If your daughter is anything like ours, she will remember these times for years to come.

TEACH HER TO
care about others.

We genuinely care for someone else when we know that person can do nothing for us, regardless of how much time, money, or other resources we invest in them. In today's "me-first" culture, genuinely caring about others is a regular casualty. With a few notable exceptions, pretty much everything around your daughter in this world will teach her to look out for #1. Don't take for granted that she will automatically care about the concerns of others.

Perhaps your daughter is already a caring person. As she gets older, however, it's possible she'll get caught up in her own interests. Life (and our natural self-focus) will produce a growing list of distractions that can drown out any genuine concern and thoughtful spirit she may have once had for others. For the Christian, the Bible is clear. Philippians 2:4 tells us we are to be genuinely concerned for and to support the interests of others. And the best way to teach this is by example. How are you going to teach your daughter by example about caring for others?

Together,
MAKE SOMETHING BEAUTIFUL
with your hands.

When I was a newly married bride, my mom signed the two of us up for quilt-in-a-day class. She happens to be an amazing seamstress, but me? Not so much. So I wasn't sure what I'd think of this quilting class. It turned out that although I wasn't a particularly gifted seamstress, I had a knack for quilting.

I not only learned to quilt in that season of my life, but I also learned something even more valuable. While I'm not a naturally "crafty" person, I realized the value and satisfaction of creating something beautiful with your hands—and doing it with someone you love.

Oh, and twenty-six years later, I still have the quilt I made in that class. It might be faded and worn, but it's still lovely to me.

So make something marvelous with your girl. You don't know what it might mean to her many years down the road.

LET YOUR DAUGHTER *know* YOU *admire* HER *intelligence*.

We want our daughters to be reflective, independent thinkers, moved by all that is right, good, and true and not swayed by the persuasive abilities of others. Your daughter has a good mind, but if this world succeeds in convincing her that she isn't intelligent, she'll exercise her mind less and less as she is swayed by the opinions of others.

By communicating that you appreciate her natural intelligence, you're directly building her up. You're also indirectly encouraging her to think and formulate her thoughts purposefully, which will further increase her intellectual powers.

So don't leave her with any doubt about how highly you admire her God-given intelligence.

Begin praying FOR HER *future husband.*

If you looked at my prayer journal, you'd see a spot with a longtime mother's prayer for a few young men I've not yet met. I don't know who they are and, as far as I can tell, my daughters don't either. But all our girls hope to marry someday, so I pray for those husbands-to-be. It's always possible that marriage won't be part of God's plan for them, but why not pray for that in case it turns out to be?

So I pray their husbands will be strong and kind. I pray God will protect them and keep them. I pray He will be preparing them, not only for marriage in general but specifically for marriage with my daughters. I pray each one will be a faithful man—faithful to his God and faithful to his wife.

Start praying for your future son-in-law now. You can never start too soon. He'll probably thank you someday. And so will she.

Encourage her TO DO THE *right thing,* NO MATTER *how hard* IT IS.

We all naturally desire to avoid hardship—especially when it is relational. Your daughter will encounter many circumstances in which the easy way out will free her from many difficult matters. But the easy way out is almost always a shortcut that brings other, worse consequences.

A young woman of character doesn't sidestep responsibility and does the right thing, even when it brings hardship.

BE *grateful* FOR YOUR *world-changer.*

So, do you have one of those girls? You know, the kind who doesn't budge—filled with passion, determination, and wild ideas. She's lovely, and you love her. But then there are those days when she has you scratching your head, maybe even crying a few tears and praying in the wee hours of the night. That kind of girl.

We get that. It's not easy being the parent of such a girl. We've raised one or two of them ourselves. We've spent—and spend—many hours on our knees for them.

But you should know something. That little (or maybe even not-so-little) girl of yours can grow up to be just the kind of woman this world needs.

Her ability to stand her ground will be beautiful when she's out there standing for what's right. Her willingness to go against the flow will be a relief when you see she's not easily swayed by the crowd. And those wild ideas will be so wonderful when she offers them to help a hurting world.

Take heart. Sometimes a world-changer looks a lot like a strong-willed girl. She may not be easy to raise, but she sure is a gift. Not only to you but to all of us.

Be grateful for your world-changer.

Applaud
HER INDIVIDUAL
choices.

One day my daughter came home with a big shock of purple hair. Everyone thought her dad would overreact (now, why would they jump to that conclusion?), but I didn't. I told her that if she liked it, I liked it too.

"I do!" she said.

"Then so do I!" I said—and I meant it.

We then took a picture together next to our elderberry shrub. I love that picture. It reminds me of a time when I did the right thing in the moment. Trust me, I've not always made the right choice in these moments.

You want to protect your daughter, and if you're like me and on high alert all the time, you need to be especially careful. The five-alarm fire siren isn't appropriate for 99 percent of the choices your daughter makes. She will make many decisions you don't agree with. In those dicey years between when she's a young woman and a full adult, it's vital that she knows you respect her as a person. To build this message into your relationship's DNA, she needs to learn, over time, that you respect her as a unique and separate person, with her own distinct likes and dislikes and her own way of seeing the world.

You can believe that the day is coming when you'll have a "purple hair" moment! It's not about the hair; it's about choosing something you wouldn't choose. If it's a destructive choice, that's one thing, but many choices will simply be her own preferences, and not the same as yours. Let your daughter know you like her and you like her choices . . . for her!

SHOW *appreciation* FOR HER *strengths* THAT ARE *different* FROM YOUR OWN.

I found myself needing some help recently—a lot of help, actually. I might be "the mom," but I needed someone with different gifts than what I've been given. We were putting on an event that required creativity and attention to detail, and I couldn't quite pull it off on my own. So I asked one of my daughters if she could give me a hand with the project.

Honestly, she became my lifesaver. I felt like a weight was lifted off my shoulders knowing she had things covered and I was free to do what I was called to do.

I didn't have this picture in mind when this talented daughter was a little girl though. Not that I didn't see her as bright and imaginative—because I did. But how could I have known that she'd grow up to offer her gifts to *me*? That her unique strengths would save the day?

If you have a daughter with strengths that are different from your own (and perhaps these "differences" even annoy you at times), you might discover that someday you'll need those differences. Or perhaps the whole world will need them.

Appreciate the strengths she's developing today and watch how God will use them in the future.

Tell her THAT YOU *value* WHAT AND *how she thinks.*

As your daughter gets older, she will begin to formulate her own thoughts and perspectives about various subjects and about the character of people she encounters. She will likely grow in maturity in these things far sooner than you realize or give her credit for.

You're a wise parent, so you'll be looking for the signs of growing maturity. You'll want to communicate to your daughter that her thoughts are valuable and make a meaningful contribution to your own thinking. When you do, you send a powerful message that you respect and have confidence in her, which will, in turn, help her continue to grow strong on the inside.

COMMUNICATE THAT
you have faith
IN HER FUTURE.

Our daughter was in her final year of college, and the uncertainty of what would come next weighed heavily on her. Should she continue to live on the East Coast or come back home to the West Coast? Should she find a stable job or take a risk with an interesting internship? We could hear the pressure in her voice when we spoke with her on the phone.

They were big life choices for a young woman.

While we didn't know what would be best for her, we told her we were confident that God had loving plans for her future. We repeated the same thing we'd said to her growing up. Every time she doubted what was next and if she was up for what lay ahead, we'd tell her, "God has you in His caring hands, and that is a very good place to be."

As parents, we can forget how scary the future can seem to a child. She wonders what's before her and if she'll be ready for it. Remind her that she's not on her own because you'll be there for her. Even better yet, God is watching over her and He will care for her.

ENJOY *your daughter* FOR *who she is* TODAY.

You're a parent, so it's challenging to think about your daughter without thinking about your hopes and dreams for her. You focus on the future and how her decisions will form the days ahead. You think about all that can be and how much you know she can achieve. It's exciting to think about the amazing woman she will be someday.

But are you living in the promise of your daughter's future rather than in the relationship you can enjoy today? Sure, tomorrow you'll definitely appreciate her company when she's older and more mature. But she's also a wonderful person right now. Your daughter needs to know that you enjoy her as she is today. She needs to know you think she's great just the way she is.

How can you do that? Don't let another day pass without telling your daughter, "I think you're awesome! I really enjoy who you are!"

Be willing
TO LET HER GO WHEN THE
time comes.

"You know that this goes against every natural instinct in my body, don't you?"

That's what I whispered to my husband as we lay on our pillows that last night before she left home. Our young adult daughter was moving clear across the country—the beginning of a new adventure for her but one that left a large hole in our lives.

It wasn't that I thought what she was doing was wrong or bad or dangerous (okay, maybe a tad dangerous since it's Washington, DC, we're talking about here). But it was so hard to let her go. So sad to say goodbye to our ray of sunshine.

Sometimes as parents, we have to make difficult choices that go against our own heart's desire and instead choose what's best for our child. We must give up a bit of our own happiness or sense of security for their sake.

So we watch, we pray, and we let go. It's a big part of parenting others forgot to tell us about. Yet we still keep trying to tell ourselves that our children are somehow "ours," and we comfort ourselves with that.

In reality, however, your daughter is a gift to treasure but not to grab. So, when the times comes, let her go with your blessing and your prayers.

ALWAYS *kiss her* GOODNIGHT.

Our twenty-year-old daughter stopped by last night for a family dinner. She was heading out of town on a business trip and wanted to say goodbye before she took off for the convention. We love that she does that, and we're grateful she calls us up and wants to come over.

It was a warm summer evening, and her dad had cooked up his famous fried chicken, so we ate outside on the back patio. It was a three-napkin meal with lots of finger licking in between—messy but amazing. And we laughed and talked together the entire time.

She didn't stay late because she had an early flight in the morning, but before she left she went around and kissed us each goodnight. First the left cheek and then the right. The way the French do it.

That's how our family has said goodnight since any of us can remember. It doesn't matter how late it is or what's going on in our lives, we always wish each other goodnight. We say goodnight and kiss both cheeks.

It made me smile to see her kissing us goodnight this time, when it was the other way around for so many years.

Maybe it looks a little different for you, but here's your chance to end the day with love and a kiss. So be sure to say goodnight to your girl and wish her sweet dreams.

Matt Jacobson is the founder of FaithfulMan.com, an online ministry encouraging readers to love God and walk faithfully according to the Word. Matt is cohost (with his wife, Lisa) of *FAITHFUL LIFE*, a weekly podcast focusing on what it means to be a biblical Christian in marriage, parenting, church, and culture.

Matt attended Multnomah University in Oregon and studied philosophy at Trinity Western University in British Columbia. For twenty-five years, Matt has been an executive in the publishing industry. For the past seventeen years, he has been pastor and elder of Cline Falls Bible Fellowship, a thriving community of Christians with a purposeful discipleship focus on marriage, family, and church leadership development. He is a biblical marriage coach and the author of the bestselling book *100 Ways to Love Your Wife*, as well as *100 Words of Affirmation Your Wife Needs to Hear*. For more information, visit FaithfulMan.com.

Lisa Jacobson studied abroad in Paris and Israel and lived in mud huts in Cameroon before marrying Matt and raising and home-educating their eight children in the Pacific Northwest. She is a graduate of Willamette

University and has an MA from Western Seminary. In 2012, Lisa began Club31Women.com, a writing, mentoring, and speaking ministry that has grown into a powerful voice for biblical womanhood. She is also the author of the bestselling books *100 Ways to Love Your Husband* and *100 Words of Affirmation Your Husband Needs to Hear*.

Matt and Lisa cohost the popular *FAITHFUL LIFE* podcast, focusing on what it means to be a biblical Christian in marriage, parenting, church, and culture.

Connect with
Lisa and *Club31Women!*

Club31Women.com

Cohost of *FAITHFUL LIFE* Podcast

@Club31Women

@FaithfulLife

@Club31Women

@Club31Women

Connect with
MATT and **FAITHFUL MAN!**

FaithfulMan.com

Cohost of *FAITHFUL LIFE* Podcast

@FaithfulMan

@FaithfulLife

@FaithfulMan

Hands-on advice
to *LOVE* one another better.

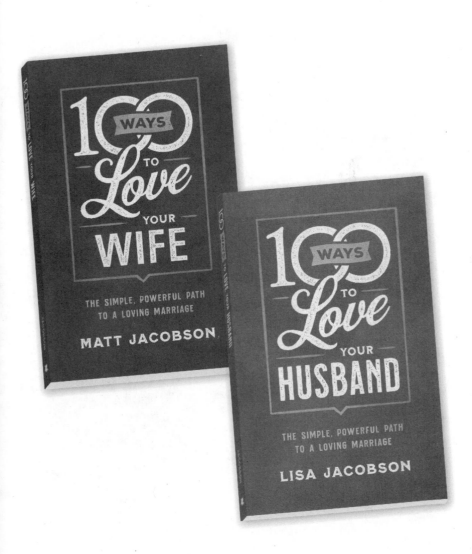

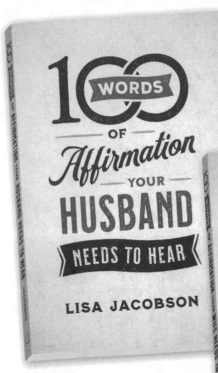